Celebrating the Fourth of July

The Child's World®
childsworld.com

Published by The Child's World®
1980 Lookout Drive • Mankato, MN 56003-1705
800-599-READ • www.childsworld.com

Photographs ©: iStockphoto, cover, 1, 14–15, 16;
Steve Debenport/iStockphoto, 4–5; Christin Lola/
Shutterstock Images, 6–7; Shutterstock Images, 9; Wave
Break Media/iStockphoto, 10; Spotmatik Ltd./Shutterstock
Images, 13; Jesus Chueca/Shutterstock Images, 18–19;
Raghu Ramaswamy/iStockphoto, 21; Red Line Editorial,
22

ISBN 9781503823785
LCCN 2017945000

Printed in the United States of America
PA02358

ABOUT THE AUTHOR

Maddie Spalding is a writer and
editor who lives in Minnesota. She
has written more than 20 books for
children. Her favorite summertime
activity is spending time with family
at their lakeside cabin.

Contents

Parade

Today is the Fourth of July! The United States became a country on this day in 1776. Americans celebrate their country.

People wear red, white, and blue. They watch a parade. They see many U.S. flags.

Trip to the Park

It is a warm day. We walk to a park.

It is time for lunch! Some people make sandwiches. They have a **picnic**.

People play baseball
in the park. Others join
the fun.

13

Cold summer treats
are tasty!

Later people eat dinner.
They grill burgers. They
eat hot dogs.

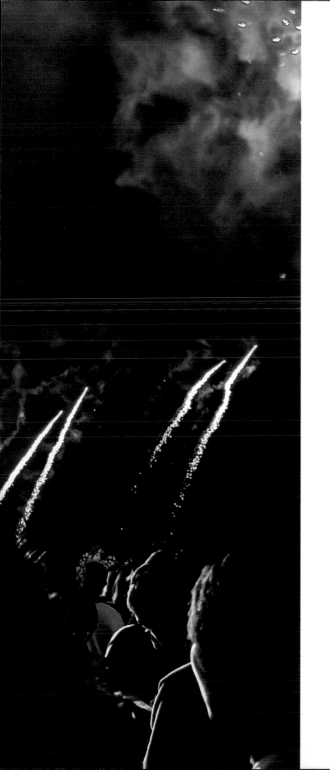

Fireworks

It gets dark. We gather on a hill. We see friends. It is time for fireworks!

We watch the sky. Look! There is a **burst** of color. The Fourth of July is my favorite summer **holiday**!

21

Straw Fireworks Painting

Make your own fireworks painting!

Supplies:

7 bendy straws   paint (many colors)
  paper plate   tape
  newspaper   white paper

Instructions:

1. Put the paper plate on the newspaper. Squirt some paint onto the plate.

2. Bend the tops of your straws. Hold all the straws together so that their bent ends form a star.

3. Tape the straws together.

4. Dip the bent ends of the straws into the paint.

5. Stamp the painted ends of the straws onto the white paper.

Glossary

burst—(BURST) A burst is a short blast. A firework is a burst of color.

holiday—(HAH-li-day) A holiday is a day when people celebrate a special occasion. The Fourth of July is an important summer holiday.

picnic—(PIK-nik) A picnic is a meal that is eaten outdoors. We have a picnic on the Fourth of July.

To Learn More

Books

Appleby, Alex. *Happy Fourth of July!*
New York, NY: Gareth Stevens, 2014.

Hayes, Amy. *Celebrate Independence
Day*. New York, NY: Cavendish Square,
2015.

Web Sites

Visit our Web site for links about
the Fourth of July:
childsworld.com/links

*Note to Parents, Teachers, and Librarians: We routinely verify
our Web links to make sure they are safe and active sites. So
encourage your readers to check them out!*

Index